"All over this nation, God is stirring the hearts of men to rise up and enter into their God-given destiny. Lou Turner's lifelong passion is to see men enter into their divine purpose in life. 'Living Life God's Way,' of which this book is a part, is born out of this passion. Throughout this Bible study series, Turner opens up God's Word to help you discover HIS plan for your success in your life, family, and work. If you are ready to get off the treadmill, to begin to enjoy God's fullness in your life and make a significant contribution to the world around you, I recommend that you dive into this life-transforming Bible study."

Hal H. Sacks, D.Min., *BridgeBuilders International Leadership Network*

"It seems North American culture is rapidly moving toward what the Bible calls 'everyone doing what is right in his own mind' (Judges 21:25). The prophet Isaiah declared, 'Woe to those who call evil, good, and good, evil' (Isaiah 5:20). This Bible study series will challenge every man in the 21st century as 'iron sharpens iron'! The Q&As at the end of each chapter really personalize the teaching."

Dennis Conner, *Co-Founder/President, Called to Serve Prayer-Coaching Ministry*

"I have known Lou Turner for over twenty years. Lou loves Jesus and has built his life on the Word of God. Lou's Bible study series, 'Living Life God's Way,' is full of biblical truth that has been tested and can be applied by disciples of Jesus in practical ways. These books will help you grow in your faith and gain confidence and competence, which will increase your fruitfulness in Christ.

Mark Buckley, *Founding Pastor of Living Streams Church*

Living Life God's Way

A MAN AND SEX

LOU TURNER

A Man and Sex
First Edition Trade Book, 2019
Copyright © 2019 by Lou Turner

A Man and Sex is part of the Living Life God's Way Series by Lou Turner.

All rights reserved. No part of this publication may be reproduced, stored in a retrieval system, or transmitted in any form by any means—electronic, mechanical, photocopy, recording, or otherwise—except for brief quotations in critical reviews or articles, without the prior permission of the publisher, except as provided by U.S. copyright law.

Unless otherwise marked, Scriptures are taken from the ESV® Bible (The Holy Bible, English Standard Version®) copyright © 2001 by Crossway Bibles, a publishing ministry of Good News Publishers. ESV Text Edition: 2016. The ESV® text has been reproduced in cooperation with and by permission of Good News Publishers. Unauthorized reproduction of this publication is prohibited. All rights reserved.

Scriptures marked NIV are taken from the Holy Bible, New International Version®, NIV®. Copyright © 1973, 1978, 1984, 2011 by Biblica, Inc.™ Used by permission of Zondervan. All rights reserved worldwide. www.zondervan.com The "NIV" and "New International Version" are trademarks registered in the United States Patent and Trademark Office by Biblica, Inc.™

Scriptures marked TLB are taken from the Living Bible, copyright © 1971. Used by permission of Tyndale House Publishers, Inc., Carol Stream, Illinois 60188. All rights reserved.

Some of the anecdotal illustrations in this book are true to life and are included with the permission of the persons involved. All other illustrations are composites of real situations, and any resemblance to people living or dead is coincidental.

ISBN: 978-1-7329092-7-4

To order additional books:
www.amazon.com
www.hislifeinus.com

Editorial and Book Packaging: Inspira Literary Solutions, Gig Harbor, WA
Book Design: PerfecType, Nashville, TN
Cover Design: MTWdesign, Dickson, TN
Printed in the USA by Ingram Spark

He will be like a tree firmly planted by streams of water,
Which yields its fruit in its season
And its leaf does not wither;
And in whatever he does, he prospers.

Psalm 1:3

TABLE OF CONTENTS

Preface   ix

How to Use This Book   xi

Introduction   xiii

1. Sex in Marriage—Blessed by God   1

2. Dealing with Challenges   15

3. What Will We Do with God's Moral Standards?   27

4. Sexual Purity: The Battleground and the Victory   45

5. Walking in Purity   55

6. Pornography   67

A Final Word   71

Appendix   73

About the Author   81

PREFACE

We live in a world that has largely forgotten what manhood is about. In the Western world, men are often portrayed on television as buffoons who are out of touch and must rely on their wives to straighten them out. These characters are portrayed as silly, insensitive, lacking common sense, and when they do speak, they are generally wrong. They are generally portrayed as either ridiculously weak or overly macho. They are not able to commit to a long-term relationship and generally mistreat women. Positive role models are hard to find in the media.

However, the Bible teaches a different type of manhood, the authentic one. Men are to be leaders, loving their wives and children, excelling in their work, and standing for truth. They are to be men of wisdom, knowledge, having godly character and seeking after God and His direction. They are to be exhibiting godly leadership at church, in the community, and in business, and to be a light to those around them. They are to be men of compassion and love, as well as courageous and bold when needed.

Men go astray from these ideals, including Christian men, due to improper convictions or beliefs about life. They have received these from various sources: well-meaning family and friends, the media, and the culture around them—a world system that promotes the tearing down of God's biblical truths.

But without proper biblical foundation, we will all go astray.

PREFACE

That's why I wrote these books, containing insights, observations, and biblical truths distilled over the course of my decades of life and ministry. Each section is designed to be a stand-alone section for study and consideration. I hope this series, *Living Life God's Way*, will be used to disciple men in biblical truths for life. Whether you use it for yourself, with a group, or to mentor or disciple someone else, my hope is that it will be a blessing to you and encourage you to seek God and grow in Him.

HOW TO USE THIS BOOK

What does it mean to be a "good" husband and father?
How do I live out the Christian life at work?
What does God want from me—and how am I supposed to find that out?

These were questions that plagued me as a young man—questions, I learned, that are at the front of many men's minds at various times in their lives. For me, these questions began my quest to seek God and discover the answers, and my discoveries, over the years of my life, led to this series of booklets, *Living Life God's Way*. The series discusses 13 topics that every man must deal with, regardless of his work, calling, profession, or circumstances. It is difficult to know how to live the Christian life without understanding what God says about these areas of life.

These topics are:

1. Seeking and Finding God
2. Who You Are in Christ
3. A Man's Work and Ministry
4. Understanding Authority
5. A Man and His Wife
6. A Man and His Children
7. Getting Guidance from God

HOW TO USE THIS BOOK

8. Overcoming Strongholds
9. A Man and Money
10. Repentance, Forgiveness, and Restitution
11. Being a Leader
12. A Man and Sex
13. The Test of Pride

You can use these books to study on your own, in a small group, or with a larger group of men. Each topic or booklet is a stand-alone study, and a person can begin with any one he chooses. They are different lengths and can be adapted to various settings—home, church, or community—all topics that are pertinent to today.

Explore what the Bible says about these important and critical areas. The encouragement is to read these with an open heart, asking God to reveal His truth to you in each of these areas of life. Pray that His Spirit will show you His truth, so that you may live in it and enjoy all God has for you. I pray that you experience the blessing and presence of God in your life as you draw closer to Him and more aware of His leading in every area of your life.

INTRODUCTION TO A MAN AND SEX

As we study the subject of a man's sexual life, we have to realize that our culture has given us a lot of false information. Since God designed sex, and gave us the path of truth regarding morality, we need to look at what *He* says about it before we come to our own conclusions.

God created sex and had a specific plan for it in our lives and relationships. He made it for good purposes for us, and it is part of the way He created us. He created both men and women with a desire for romance, connection, and sexual intimacy. These are a part of our nature.

Sadly, many couples do not experience the best of this in their relationship. While most men and women openly (or secretly) desire a loving, intimate marriage, many do not actually experience it. Because of past hurts both in and outside of marriage—as well as erroneous or warped ideas of what a physical relationship is supposed to be like—many couples do not have the loving, fulfilling, and exciting relationship God intends for them.

We should be free in our marriages to express our desire and love for our spouse. We should take delight in each other. Unfortunately, Satan has worked hard to distort God's intention for marriage and physical intimacy. But when we know and understand the truth of God's Word regarding sex and marriage, we can choose to walk in His design and enjoy the blessings of physical intimacy.

That is the focus of this volume of the "Living Life God's Way" Men's Series. Bottom line: if we want to understand the intention for sex and enjoy it appropriately, we must look to the One who made it, to discover and fully appreciate its proper purpose in our lives.

Chapter 1

SEX IN MARRIAGE—BLESSED BY GOD

Different cultures all have their own thoughts, desires, and philosophies about sex. What is "acceptable" is different depending on where you go. But let's face it, sex is everywhere: on TV, in advertising, in the movies, and basically everywhere else around us. The exposure is getting more graphic and more explicit and bombarding our minds and hearts. This appeals to our natural physical and sexual nature, but takes it to a level that is unhealthy. Nevertheless, God created sex and had a specific—and very good!—plan for it in our lives. In this volume of the "Living Life God's Way" series, we're going to look to Him and His Word to discover the appropriate place for, and expression of, our sexuality.

God's Good Plan

Every generation of teenagers thinks it is discovering sex for the first time in human history; many get caught up in sexual activities and some become obsessed. Different cultures all have their own thoughts, desires, and philosophies about sex. What is "acceptable" is different depending on where you go. The reality is that God always intended for the sexual relationship between a husband and wife to be a place of pleasure and intimacy.

God originally made man and woman exactly the way He intended. Scripture records that after He finished His creation, *"God saw everything He had made, and indeed it was very good"* (Genesis 1:31). "Very good" included being pleased with the way He made man and woman *sexually*.

The union between a man and woman in marriage is unique in all of creation. Later in the Genesis creation story, there is a commentary on what happens when a man and woman marry: *"Therefore a man shall leave his father and mother and be joined to his wife, and they shall become one flesh"* (Genesis 2:24).

God intended man and woman to enter into a lifelong relationship in which they would learn to love each other, share life with each other, help each other, and glorify God by fulfilling His purpose for them. According to Genesis 1:28, they were to be fruitful and multiply, take dominion over the earth, and enjoy God's creation.

However, Satan wanted to corrupt God's perfect creation, including the relationship between a husband and wife. He immediately went to work. His chief method was lying and trying to convince man and woman to distrust God. Satan deceived Eve and convinced her to doubt God and to disobey Him. She in turn persuaded Adam to enter into disobeying God and doubting Him. In this way, sin entered the world. Since that time, Satan has continued to war against God's purpose in every area of life, including marriage and sexual intimacy.

A Picture of God's Design

To begin to see past Satan's distortions to God's original design, we need to look at God's view of the sexual relationship between a man and woman. One of the books of the Bible that displays this in detail is the Song of Solomon.

The Song of Solomon is a poetic love story between two people. It shows their desire to be together, to share their love, and even to show their delight in each other physically.

Many people have taught that this book is simply an allegory showing the relationship between Christ and the Church. That may certainly be part of it. However, it is also strong evidence of how God made men and women with strong sexual drives. To take the position that He would have little to say to us about that is not only illogical, it's impractical. The Bible is full of practical teaching about every area of life, including sex.

When a man and woman are in love, they want to marry and express their love for each other in a physical manner. This is natural and normal; it's what God intended.

In Song of Solomon, both the man and the woman, as husband and wife, sought each other out, longed for each other's love, and delighted in each other's physical attributes. They were excited about each other and being together. Again, this is the way God desires it to be.

This desire to be together has a side benefit. Learning to love our wives unconditionally, and learning to love each other romantically and physically, helps us understand God's love for us. As we grow in our love for each other, and learn to delight in each other, it becomes easier to understand how God loves us.

One thing that stands out in the Song of Solomon is that the wife (or the "Shulamite" in the story) seeks out her husband for love as much as he seeks her (Song of Solomon 3:1-4). They both have the freedom to express their love and desire, and their delight in their relationship is free and unashamed. Put in more popular vernacular: Both of them took the opportunity to "make the first move," so to speak!

> **One thing we need to establish is that
> both men and women
> desire romance
> and have a deep need for it.
> Men do not need it more than women.**

Sadly, many couples do not have this type of relationship. While most men and women desire a loving, intimate marriage, many do not actually experience it. Because of past hurts both in and outside of marriage—as well as erroneous or warped ideas of what marriage or the physical relationship is supposed to be—many couples do not have the loving, caring, and exciting relationship God intends for them. (This could be for a variety of reasons: fear in expressing oneself, past hurts and injustices, feeling unable to communicate needs openly, and so on.)

We should be free in our marriages to express our desire, our love, and to delight in each other without any shame, guilt, or fear of judgment. Unfortunately, Satan has worked hard to distort God's intention for physical intimacy. That's why we must look to God to fully enjoy the blessing of physical connection.

TAKE A BREAK

At this point, take a break, open your Bible, and read the Song of Solomon. Before you start, ask God's Spirit to reveal His desire for your marriage and your physical relationship with your spouse. If you are single, this book will show you how God intends the marriage relationship to be. After you have finished, we will look at some other scriptures that shed light on this vital aspect of the marriage relationship.

Song of Solomon paints a glorious picture of what God designed a husband and wife to experience together. Let's look at a couple more passages that talk of God's expectations for a couple's sexual relationship.

Being Faithful to Your Wife and Delighting in Her

Proverbs 5 talks about faithfulness in marriage and taking delight in your wife. The chapter opens with a strong warning, urging us to stay away from immoral relationships, stating that a man will pay a price if he pursues them.

In the Bible, immoral relationships are any sexual relationships a man or woman has outside of marriage. This chapter clearly states that a man is to completely abstain from any immoral relationships, whether he is single or married. Proverbs 5:18-20 says,

> *"Let your fountain be blessed and rejoice in the wife of your youth. As a loving deer and a graceful doe, let her breasts satisfy you at all times, and always be enraptured with her love. For why should you, my son, be enraptured by an immoral woman, and be embraced in the arms of a seductress?"*

Here we clearly see the Bible stating that our "sexual fountain" (our sexuality) will be blessed by God when we share it only with our wife.

In numerous other passages, the Bible teaches that a sexual relationship is only to be between a man and a woman. We will see this multiple times as we go through this study. For example, Jesus stated,

> *"Have not you read that He who made them at the beginning made them male and female, and said, 'For this reason a man shall leave his father and mother and be joined to his wife, and the two shall become one flesh'? So then, they are no longer two but one flesh. Therefore what God has joined together, let not man separate"* (Matthew 19:4-6).

This passage points out that God ordained marriage to be between one man and one woman and issued a warning that no one should try to separate them.

The Bible also states there is a price to pay for being involved in immoral relationships:

> *Remove your way far from her* (speaking to the temptation of immorality) *and do not go near the door of her house, lest you give your honor to others, and your years to the cruel one; lest aliens be filled with your wealth, and your labors go to the house of a foreigner; and you mourn at last, when your flesh and your body are consumed, and say; "How I have hated instruction, and my heart despised reproof! I have not obeyed the voice of my teachers, nor inclined my ear to those who instructed me! I was on the verge of total ruin, in the midst of the congregation and assembly."* (Proverbs 5:8-14)

The writer of the above passages in Proverbs states that a man's relationship with his wife is blessed by God and he is to guard himself from being involved sexually with anyone outside of marriage. *"Drink water from your own cistern, and running water from you own well,"* he says. *"Should your fountains be dispersed abroad, streams of water in the streets? Let them be only your own, and not for strangers with you"* (Proverbs 5:15-17).

Many married men have suffered this kind of ruin because of unfaithfulness to their wives. They have gone through divorce, their wealth or resources have gone to others, their children are wounded, and their families decimated.

Single men pay a price for immorality as well. Their bodies may bear the price from a sexually transmitted disease. And years of their lives may be wasted on unfruitful relationships along with the wounds and disappointments of failed relationships. Months and even years can be lost in these failed relationships.

Thriving in Your Relationship with Your Wife

If God gave us sex to enjoy, then it certainly stands to reason it should be something a husband and wife enjoy regularly. Being sexually intimate nurtures affection, closeness, openness, romance, and other aspects of our physical and non-physical relationship. In fact, the New Testament even gives clear instructions regarding the intimate relationship between a husband and wife:

> *The husband should fulfill his marital duty to his wife, and likewise the wife to her husband. The wife does not have authority over her own body but yields it to her husband. In the same way, the husband does not have authority over his own body but yields it to his wife. Do not deprive each other except perhaps by mutual consent and for a time, so that you may devote yourselves to prayer. Then come together again so that Satan will not tempt you because of your lack of self-control.* (1 Corinthians 7:3-5)

This passage is quite clear and practical. Husbands and wives are to enjoy their sexual relationship; they are not to abstain from it except for an agreed-upon time of prayer and fasting. Neither the husband nor the wife is to use sex to manipulate, control, or deprive the other. Sex is not a weapon or a negotiating item. It is to express our love and to share intimacy.

This physical relationship falls into place based on the health of the couple's emotional relationship. If husbands are not treating their wives in a loving manner, it is difficult for their wives to respond physically. Women want to be loved, respected, listened to, valued, and cherished. Who doesn't? If a wife doesn't feel that she matters, or if she does not feel fully appreciated, she may not be "in the mood" to engage in physical intimacy.

First Peter 3:7 demonstrates that God takes the way husbands treat wives seriously:

> *Likewise you husbands, dwell with them [wives] with understanding, giving honor to the wife, as to the weaker vessel, and as being heirs together of the grace of life, that your prayers may not be hindered. Finally, all of you be of one mind, having compassion for one another; love as brothers, be tenderhearted, be courteous, not returning evil for evil, or reviling for reviling, but on the contrary blessing, knowing that you were called to this, that you may inherit a blessing.* (1 Peter 3:7-9)

God is so concerned about marriage that when a husband mistreats his wife, his prayers may be hindered! Certainly, if a man has a pattern of mistreating his wife, his prayers and relationship with both his wife and God will be affected. God loves our wives and expects us to as well.

In this passage, Peter says we are to be "tenderhearted, courteous, and not reviling." In other words, we are not to have a hostile, domineering, mean-spirited, or argumentative nature. Who wants to be around a person like that? Many men think they have to "make" their wives respect them. So, they become harsh, short-tempered, demanding, and unloving. Then they wonder why their wives don't respond to them as they desire.

When we treat our wives in a loving manner—with kindness, gentleness, compassion, and warmth, honoring the gifts they are—they will naturally want to spend time with us and share their love with us. But if we are harsh, short tempered, or simply do not make them feel important to us, they may withdraw emotionally and become unresponsive or disinterested.

We cannot treat our wives with disrespect or in a cold or demanding manner and expect them to want to respond to us physically. It is interesting that wives who have pursued affairs with other men have stated that those men made them feel special and important. They felt like the "other man" listened to them and was truly interested in them as a person (whereas their husband did not).

Do we want our marriage to be blessed? Then we must practice the principles God has given us in His Word. Consider the Song of Solomon. Look at how both the husband and wife loved, respected, and desired each other. This type of relationship takes time and effort to develop. But it is worth the effort. The payoff is great!

If you are guilty of creating an atmosphere in the home that does not foster a loving relationship, stop now! Look at the relationship from your wife's point of view and be honest about your actions. How do you speak to her? How do you speak to your children? Do you listen to her? Do you share openly? Are you attentive to her needs? Pray and ask God to reveal how He views your relationship with your wife and where you can make changes personally.

If after prayer, the Lord convicts you of mistreating your wife or not loving her as you should, confess your shortcomings to God. Ask Him to make you aware of your motivations and show you how to become the husband He desires you to be. Then you need to confess those shortcomings to your wife and ask her to forgive you. Ask her how your actions and attitudes have affected her. Purpose, with God's help, to begin to treat your wife in a loving manner.

Since He wants you to have a great relationship with your wife, He will respond and reveal the things you need to know. Remember, *"You shall know the truth, and the truth shall make your free"* (John 8:32). God wants to reveal truth to you, including regarding your relationship with your wife. If you want a close, loving, relationship with your wife, you need to practice the things that will bring it to pass.

How to Love Your Wife

No discussion on love would be complete without considering 1 Corinthians 13, also known as the "love chapter." During a time when I was praying for my wife, God impressed on me to memorize this chapter. It was the first time I'd tried to memorize an entire chapter in the Bible. Since it was only thirteen verses, I decided I could do it.

As I memorized and meditated on these verses, I began to get many insights on the true meaning of love. My perspective on loving my wife (and others) began to change. Many times, as I lay in bed at night, I would quote the verses to myself and think about the meaning of specific words. God's Spirit would provide insightful ways that I could apply these to my relationship with my wife. It changed my thinking about the true meaning of love!

It is well worth your time to study this chapter and even memorize it, so its meaning can go deep into your heart and soul. It can be life changing, I promise you! I challenge you to memorize this chapter and spend time dwelling on its application on your own life. Below is how this chapter describes love, applied to your wife. If you are not married but are dating, consider: Am I ready to love this woman in these ways?

- *Love is kind.* You take your wife's feelings and opinions into consideration.
- *Love does not envy.* You are not motivated by envy of others. You do not envy others' marriages or their wives, which could lead to covetousness or lust. You love your wife unselfishly.
- *Love does not parade itself; is not puffed up.* You are not motivated by pride; you do not let pride keep you from serving your wife. Pride can cause us to be harsh, judgmental, condescending, and demanding. When we love someone, we cannot treat them that way.
- *Love does not behave rudely.* You treat your wife with respect at all times, whether in her presence or when you speak of her in her absence.
- *Love does not seek its own.* You do not act in a self-centered or selfish manner, but want what is best for your wife and your marriage.
- *Love is not easily provoked.* You are patient with your wife.
- *Love thinks no evil.* You do not have a critical attitude toward your wife.
- *Love does not rejoice in iniquity.* You do not take pleasure in wrongdoing in your marriage.

- *Love rejoices in the truth.* You love the truth about yourself, your wife, and your marriage. More than that, you seek the truth and ask God to reveal it to you regarding your marriage and your relationship with your wife. Ask God for His perspective.
- *Love bears all things.* Under pressure and difficult circumstances, you act with patience and trust in God for the outcome.
- *Love hopes all things.* You always hope the best for your wife and marriage; your trust is in God and His goodness.
- *Love endures all things.* You endure hard times without getting bitter or becoming mean-spirited.
- *Love never fails.* Your love for your wife and your attitude of support does not fail. You learn to love her unconditionally.

This chapter serves as a reminder and a way to check ourselves to see if we are walking in love. As you memorize this chapter and think on these traits, asking God for insight, understanding, and wisdom.

Loving your wife does not mean you are weak.* A man of strength, a whole man, can defer when needed; he can admit when he is wrong. He doesn't do it because he is weak. He does so when it is the right thing to do. He does not compromise when he shouldn't—when it is the wrong thing to do. In either case, his actions and attitudes are based on love for his wife and family and desiring to honor the Lord.

We need to set the atmosphere and tone of our marriage by honoring our wives. We need to communicate with them, listen to them, understand them, and love them. A woman needs to feel valued. She needs to know, in her heart, that she is accepted and cherished, no matter what. She must feel secure in her relationship with her husband. If she knows you love her, and your

---

* See the study in this series, *A Man and His Wife*

intention is to do what is best for her and the family, it will be easier for her to trust you and follow your leadership.

God intends for a husband and wife to love each other, delight in each other, and grow in their love through all of life's circumstances, even the tough ones. Today, after decades of marriage, I love my wife in a way I was incapable of when we first married. I loved her then, but as life has gone on and we have prayed together and stuck together, our love has grown into something beyond our initial love.

QUESTIONS FOR REFLECTION AND DISCUSSION

1. How do you delight in your wife?

   _____
   _____
   _____

2. Do you consider your intimate relationship with your wife to be good and fulfilling? If so, why? If not, why not?

   _____
   _____
   _____

3. Do you think your wife would think your intimate relationship is good and fulfilling? Is she satisfied? (If you don't know, ask her.)

   _____
   _____
   _____

4. Do you pray about this area of your relationship with your wife? If you haven't considered praying about your sexual relationship with her, why do you think that is?

_____

_____

_____

5. Do both you and your wife pursue each other sexually? Are there any areas of hesitation or hurt here that you need to bring before God?

_____

_____

_____

TAKE A KNEE

Let's kneel before the Lord and pray. If you are not physically able to kneel, then kneel in your heart to the Lord. *"Father, I want my relationship with my wife to be great in every area, including our sex life. Teach me and enlighten me in this area. Show me how to love my wife. I pray that Your love for her will flow through me and that I can love her as she needs to be loved.*

Reveal any area where my motives or my thinking are wrong. Help me to be the husband, friend, and lover my wife needs me to be. Make my relationship with my wife all You want it to be—in every area. Prompt me to pray about this as often as needed. Open my heart to hear what You have to say. Thank You that You care about my marriage and have a plan for it. Show me how to do my part to make my marriage a great one."

Chapter 2

DEALING WITH CHALLENGES

Sometimes a couple's relationship is not a source of pleasure for one or both spouses. It can be painful or frustrating for them to hear of God's good plan for physical intimacy, because it is so far from what they experience. As I have discipled men over the years, I have heard some stories from some men of their longings and frustrations regarding their sexual relationships with their wives. I am always sad when I hear these types of stories because I know they are not God's desire for these couples.

In the previous chapter, we talked of the type of relationship that sets the foundation for a good sexual relationship. If that foundation is not present, it will be difficult to create an enjoyable sexual relationship. But even if a man is following God's plan for loving His wife and being faithful to her, there can still be problems.

Following are a few of the reasons one spouse or the other may be struggling:

Lack of Sexual Fulfillment

Some spouses may not enjoy their sexual relationship because of a lack of satisfaction. They may be frustrated or unfulfilled. I am not talking of when a spouse might feel frustrated with the other for not engaging in a sexual act one wants and the other does not. I am speaking of normal sexual satisfaction where both spouses enjoy the act of making love and look forward to doing it again.

The question of finding sexual fulfillment in marriage brings up a number of foundational issues:

- Can a person find long-term sexual fulfillment in just one person?
- Can each spouse consistently be sexually fulfilled by the other?
- Can two people find their sexual life exciting and fulfilling long term?

The answer to all of these questions is *yes*.

Proverbs 3 speaks of a man being delighted in his wife and satisfied with her always. Why would God say such a thing unless it was true and able to be achieved? Committing to love someone for life and learning to love them deeply and romantically is God's plan. The problem is that the world's ideas have become so entrenched in Christians' thinking, that often they have bought into lies about love between a man and a woman.

Because of a lack of fulfillment, some people fantasize about others and allow their thoughts and feelings to infiltrate their minds. Many actually believe this is normal. I have even heard of pastors who counseled couples to view pornography to stimulate their feelings and responses to each other. But sin is never God's way to solve problems. Pornography is sin and it ruins marriages. It **never** helps. While pornography may stir sexual passion, it does not touch the real cause of the problem, which is a lack of the love God wants us to have for our spouse.

Other people feel a lack of fulfillment in their marriage because one spouse desires sex more frequently than the other. I have met a few men who feel they need to have sexual relations with their wife daily, or even several times a day. While this may work for some couples, it is unrealistic for most. Energy levels affect physical desires, and making it a daily routine, can take the romance out of it. "Often" or "regular" needs to be defined by both spouses. If a couple desires daily sexual activity, then that is fine. But if one or both cannot maintain that pace, then the other needs to understand and compromise. Remember, we are talking about making love and enjoying each other, not just a daily physical act to keep one spouse happy.

If your sexual relationship is unsatisfying for you or you wife, begin to pray about it. While this idea may be foreign to some people, God made and ordained this part of our relationship and has a plan for it. As you pray over your relationship with your spouse, God will give you insight and understanding. I can only tell you it is well worth the effort and time in prayer to see God work in your marriage, in every area, including your sexual relationship with your wife.

One night, while in prayer, God quickened the thought to me that human love, by itself, is inadequate. In other words, I can only love someone to the extent of my ability to love. God began to impress upon me that He wanted to add His love to mine and love my wife through me, and He wanted to love me through my wife.

I thought I was doing a pretty good job of loving my wife. But God wanted me to experience more. He wanted to get involved in my relationship with my wife in a greater way. He wanted her to experience His love for her through me and for me to experience His love for me through her. This thought may be foreign to you, but the Bible says, "God is love" (1 John 4:8). God wants us to experience His love in a greater way. One of those ways is through our relationship with our wife. Yes, God wants to be involved in our sex life with our wife! It's kind of a revolutionary thought, but it's true.

I was impressed that I should begin praying for God's supernatural and unconditional love for my wife to be released in me, and flow through me to her. I shared this with Joan, and we both began to pray for God's love to be released in us for the other. Our love and relationship went to a new level. As I have continued to pray for this over the years, I have found love for her increasing, as well as excitement at being married to her and having her for my wife. This is a powerful prayer for a man to pray over his marriage. Getting God's love involved in our relationship with our wife will always take it to a new level, a better one.

Physical Problems

Many types of physical problems can affect the ability to be physically intimate with our mates. I have known a number of couples in which the wife had a complete hysterectomy, resulting in a drastically lowered ability to produce the hormones needed to be sexually active.

Numerous other conditions can affect a couple's sexual life. In most cases, however, the underlying conditions can be remedied. Many women who have a reduced hormone level may have a reaction to synthetic hormones, but do well with bio-identical

DEALING WITH CHALLENGES

hormones. Also, as people age, their bodies change and the ability to be sexually active changes, depending on the couple and their physical state. Many couples are able to be sexually active into their 80s, while others are not.

Regardless of the physical problem, it is important to seek God for His healing or His solution. It may come through a doctor or something or someone else. Many times, He will reveal a natural course for healing. Vitamins and minerals, exercise, and proper eating can cure a multitude of physical conditions. We need to understand that we are the caretakers of our bodies. If we mistreat or abuse them, we will get sick or begin to have physical problems.

Weight gain (in either husband or wife) is another type of physical problem that causes issues with intimacy. For some couples, being overweight may not be a problem. For others, it may be an issue. For couples for whom it does cause difficulty, there is a duality of responsibility.

First, we are to love our mates unconditionally. Making an overweight spouse feel unloved and full of guilt and shame is not God's way. This is a problem the husband and wife should tackle together. Second, we are each responsible to take care of our own bodies. This includes exercise, eating properly, getting the vitamins and minerals we need, getting proper rest, and using common sense regarding our health.

Let me recommend you talk to your spouse about this. Be open and honest but not mean or accusing. Discuss the problem and agree to take practical action. Then, start doing what you've talked about.

Also, ask God to show you His will in this area. If you have a problem with food, whether overeating or a poor diet, begin to ask God to change your heart's desires, your thinking (get your mind renewed in this area of life), and your attitude about food and eating. If this is a real stronghold in your life, then you should pray over it daily, trusting God to help you make the needed changes. If you are serious, He will. If you need to, ask Him to give you the desire to change; to change your heart about the type of food you eat.

We live in a society where far too many people are sick, tired, and overweight. We cannot expect God to give us His best if we are unwilling to do our part. This does not mean we become obsessed with having a perfect body or spend hours a day in the gym. Rather, we should take this area of life seriously and be a good caretaker of our health. We should want to keep ourselves healthy and fit for our spouse, as well as for ourselves.

Past Hurts

When it comes to experiencing freedom in showing physical love to our spouse, past hurts from sexual abuse, immoral relationships, and emotional wounds from members of the opposite sex, as well as emotional wounds from family members, can all have an effect. Many people are ruled by these hurts; their actions, thoughts, and the condition of their hearts revolve around wounds they have experienced.

If long-standing wounds are keeping either you or your wife from being able to freely show love and respond sexually, then you must realize and acknowledge there is a problem. God wants to heal you, so you can enjoy the relationship He intends you to have with your spouse.

The place to begin is prayer. Tell your problem to the Lord and ask Him to heal you. I would recommend daily prayer about this until God begins to give you insight. You must be willing to admit there is a problem, accept responsibility to deal with it, and seek Him with an open heart. Remember, James 1: 5-8 promises that He will give us wisdom if we ask Him for it.

The road to healing starts as you begin to take steps in the direction God leads. Perhaps counseling will help; however, please make sure the counseling is biblically based. If a wife has been hurt in this area, her husband can show leadership by the following:

1. ***Praying for his wife.*** The best thing he can do for her is intercede for her. He should ask God to give him, and her, insight as well as direction for healing.
2. ***Being willing to listen to her experience and what she is dealing with.*** He needs to be patient, compassionate, and understanding. If a wife has been gravely hurt, she may need to process more deeply or widely than her husband is able to go with her, and he will need to help her find a trusted mentor or a counselor. This should include praying with her about it, several times a week if possible.
3. ***If counseling is needed, helping her find it and freeing up money for it.*** Make sure the counseling is biblically based and that the counselor will recommend solutions that agree with Scripture. A counselor who doesn't believe in prayer and the power of the Holy Spirit is probably not be the right choice. Past hurts cannot be healed by drugs or by intellectual reasoning alone.
4. ***If unforgiveness is an issue, working with his wife through prayer and Bible study*** regarding forgiveness to help her move toward being able to forgive the offender. *
5. ***Loving his wife, being supportive, valuing her, and making her feel secure*** in her relationship with him.

---

* For further study on forgiveness read the section in this series entitled, *Forgiveness, Restitution, and Repentance.*

Lack of Understanding of God's Plan for Intimacy

In many marriages, a couple's beliefs or mindsets can affect their sexual relationship. One or both of the spouses may simply not understand God's plan for sexual intimacy. They may have a hard time believing they are to enjoy this part of their relationship freely and openly. Many may even feel guilty for enjoying sexual relations or feel there is something wrong if they do. These inhibitions, which are not of the Lord, hold them back and rob them of God's best.

On the other hand, past sexual experiences, or involvement in pornography, can create unrealistic expectations of what intimacy and sexuality should look like.

There is a great deal of sexual perversion in the world. Not all sexual acts are proper, and it is wrong to try to convince or even force your wife to do things she is uncomfortable with in the name of "overcoming inhibitions."

While there should be freedom to express love physically and please each other, we must not enter into selfishness in a sexual relationship. Forcing your wife into any sexual act is not loving her; it is using her. If a man concentrates on loving his wife and trying to please and satisfy her, it will normally result in her desiring to do the same.

Again, read and think about the scriptures we've covered, such as Song of Solomon. Read them with your spouse and ask God to free both of you from any misconceptions. Ask for His love to fill this arena and for Him to love your spouse through you with a supernatural love. Ask Him to help you to be unashamed to show physical love with your wife, and pray this with your wife as well. As you do this, watch what God will do.

An Unloving, Hard-hearted, or Contentious Spouse

Sometimes, a wife holds back from freely expressing love—not just physically, but also emotionally. It is difficult for a husband to freely show love to someone who is hard-hearted or contentious. A heart change is necessary here before a real relationship change can take place, and only God can change a heart. If you think your wife fits in this category, seek God for His solution. But first, you must open your heart to God and allow Him to change you, first.

I have spoken with men who have told me that they were having marital problems. When I looked into it deeper, I discovered that in some cases the wife was reacting to a husband who had treated her harshly for years. In other marriages, a pattern had been established that left the wife feeling unloved or neglected. In some cases, the husband was a workaholic and the wife felt she had to go out and establish her own life. When he decided it was time to change, she wasn't ready.

My point is that a husband needs to be open as to *why* the problem exists (and be willing to accept they could be a part of the problem). God may have to change the husband before the marriage can become what it should be.

As a godly man, it is your place to seek God for the solution, allowing Him to speak to you first while you are praying for change in the marriage. As God changes you, it often brings about change in your wife. Godly, biblically based counseling can help here as well. Most men find it hard to seek counsel, especially in the area of sex, but input from men with insight, experience, and greater knowledge can be a Godsend.

God Will Work

While the above areas we have covered may not be an exhaustive list, they offer a good beginning. A husband and wife should talk about their sexual life and if there are problems, pray over them—both together and separately.

Prayer and fasting may be necessary as you set aside special time to hear from the Lord. While you cannot change your wife, you can seek God for her and pray for Him to act on your behalf, as well as hers. You must be prepared to act as well.

In Isaiah 58, God spoke to the people who were scrupulous about fasting but at the same time were living as they wished and oppressing others: *"Is this not the fast that I have chosen,"* God said, *"to loose the bonds of wickedness, to undo the heavy burdens, to let the oppressed go free, and that you break every yoke?"* (Isaiah 58:6).

God desires that all oppressions be broken, all wickedness (areas of sin) in your life be conquered, and all heavy burdens and yokes be overcome. He wants you to be free! That is the abundant life He has promised.

Be assured, this is God's will for you, your spouse, and your marriage. He is waiting to give it to you and wants you to walk in freedom. He desires for you to have peace, love, and joy in your marriage. He wants you to delight in your marriage and your spouse. He wants to change your life and marriage to conform to His plan and purpose.

QUESTIONS FOR REFLECTION AND DISCUSSION

1. Do you think any of the problems we've discussed in this chapter, or the previous one, exist in your marriage? If so, mark the ones below that resonate with you. Also consider

showing this list to your wife and asking if any of them are true for her.
- __ Lack of delighting myself only in my wife and seeking her out
- __ Lack of a loving relationship
- __ Lack of sexual fulfillment
- __ Physical problems
- __ Past hurts
- __ Lack of understanding God's plan for intimacy
- __ An unloving, hard-hearted, or contentious spouse
- __ Other _____

2. If there are problem areas, what are you going to begin to do to improve things?

_____
_____
_____
_____

3. Do you truly believe God wants you to have a great sexual relationship with your wife, and that He is interested in helping you cultivate it? Please consider this question from His perspective and write down what you think He would want to say to you about this.

_____
_____
_____
_____

TAKE A KNEE

Let's pray: *"Dear Father, I realize that I am responsible for creating a loving, caring relationship in my marriage and home. Please begin to show me all You desire about my relationship with my wife. Give me wisdom and insight regarding any problems that exist in my marriage and my sexual relationship with her. Change my heart and renew my thinking in this area as it needs to be changed. I desire Your best. Help me to be able to discuss these issues openly and honestly with my wife, being sensitive to her feelings in these areas. I pray for the power of Your Holy Spirit to move upon me and enlighten me and give me understanding. Thank You that You care about every area of my life."*

Chapter 3

WHAT WILL WE DO WITH GOD'S MORAL STANDARDS?

No study on sex would be complete without looking at God's moral standard. As we saw at the beginning of this study, God designed sex and says it is a very good thing. It plays a powerful role in forging a one-flesh bond between a husband and wife, and in bringing new life into the world. God blesses sex within His design. The Bible is very clear: He intended for the sexual relationship to be between a man and woman in marriage. That is what He ordained and blesses.

As men, we must realize that God has a standard for sexual expression. This raises a choice for us: Will we embrace God's standard? Or will we allow society to define our moral standards? This pertains not only to what we practice, but what we think of as normal or acceptable.

What does God say is the proper standard regarding sexual activity outside of marriage? We could sum it up in one word:

purity. God wants us to abstain from any sexual participation outside of that between a husband and wife. While there may be a level of pleasure and enjoyment in having a sexual relationship with someone outside of marriage, it can ultimately lead to hurt and heartache, and will affect our relationship with God and our future spouse.

God's Standard

Let us look at some biblical terms for further understanding.

Fornication

The word *fornication* in the Bible comes from two Greek words, *porneia* and *pornos* (from which we get the word *pornography*). These words refer to "acts of immorality, sexual immorality, involved in fornication, or an immoral person." Biblically speaking, fornication is any act of sex outside of marriage. This doesn't just mean sexual intercourse. Any sex act of any kind outside of marriage is fornication.

Adultery

Adultery means a married person being involved sexually with someone other than his or her spouse. Scripture is clear about adultery. Here are some strong words in Galatians:

> *Now the works of the flesh are evident, which are: adultery, fornication, uncleanness, licentiousness, idolatry, sorcery, hatred, contentions, jealousies, outbursts of wrath, selfish ambitions, dissensions, heresies, envy, murders, drunkenness, revelries and the like; of which I tell you beforehand, just as I*

also told you in time past, that those who practice such things will not inherit the kingdom of God. (Galatians 5:19)

Adultery destroys families, marriages, and greatly affects our relationship with God.

Sexual Immorality

In the Book of Acts, the apostles wrote to the churches outside of Jerusalem and admonished them not to tolerate or be involved in acts of sexual immorality: *"We write to them to abstain from things polluted by idols, from sexual immorality . . ."* (Acts 15:20; see also 21:25). Immorality is similar to fornication; it is any sexual act with someone other than your spouse. Let's consider a couple of words that depict sexual immorality.

Lust. Romans 7 says, *"But sin, taking opportunity by the commandment, produced in me all manner of evil desire. For apart from the law sin was dead"* (verse 8). The Greek word for "evil desire" here is translated elsewhere as "lust." It refers to a strong craving for something, whether sexual or otherwise.

We need to practice self-control and not allow anything to control us, including lust. We also must not stir up these kinds of desires in others. As a Christian man, we must determine to live by God's standards and not by the world's standards. Remember, the world's standards are usually contrary to God's Word. When you are involved in sexual sin with another person, you will be guilty of enticing that person into sin. Read and consider Matthew 18:6-10, where Jesus talks of the seriousness of leading others to stumble.

Lasciviousness or Licentiousness. The Apostle Paul described people who didn't know God and were *"alienated from the life of*

God because of the ignorance that is in them, because of the hardening of their heart." He said they, "being past feeling, have given themselves over to licentiousness, to work all uncleanness with greediness" (Ephesians 4:17-19).

To be *lascivious* or *licentious* means to throw off restraint and give yourself to that which is improper. This can manifest itself in people's behavior, the way they dress, or their mode of life. Men or women who dress in revealing clothes in order to stir up sensual desires in others, or make others attracted to them physically, are being licentious. The Bible tells us not to dress in a sensual manner.

It takes faith and trust in God to believe that He will lead us to the one He has for us by seeking Him and trying to please Him in all areas of life. Trusting God to bring the right person to us is a better bet than the person we might get by other means. This does not mean we will not be attracted to the opposite sex. It does mean we keep this under control until marriage.

Homosexuality or Sodomy

Romans 1:20-32 declares that when we forsake God and His truth, deception begins to grip our hearts, and we begin to be deceived and believe lies. The list of things that come about from rejecting God's truth includes homosexuality (sometimes also called sodomy in the Bible):

> For even their women exchanged the natural use for what is against nature. Likewise, also the men, leaving the natural use of the woman, burned in their lust for one another, men with men committing what is shameful, and receiving in themselves the penalty of their error which was due.
> (Romans 1:26-27)

There is great confusion today regarding homosexuality. People have come to believe they were born with same-sex attraction, and they can do nothing about it. There have been reports of physiological findings supporting this. However, exhaustive research has been conducted in this area that confirms there is no biological basis for a person to be a homosexual. There is no "gay gene."

Many Christians and non-Christians alike are confused and have been led to believe people are born gay. Certainly, if God had created some people to be homosexuals, then how could He call the lifestyle sin? He did not create anyone with a propensity for a certain sin. (See the Appendix in this book for more on this topic.)

The Bible is clear: homosexual sex, like other sexual practices we have talked about here, is outside God's plan. Because there is so much advocacy around this issue today, it is imperative that a Christian decide his viewpoint on this: Will we accept God's standard, or will we compromise? That is the question the Church has always faced in areas related to morality.

The Pull toward Compromise

The opening chapters of the Book of Revelation record messages to the churches in Asia Minor. The message to the church in Pergamos is especially sobering for us today.

In this message, the Lord addresses certain things He has against them—things they have accepted and allowed to become a part of the church.

> *But I have a few things against you, because you have there those who hold the doctrine of Balaam, who taught Balak to put a stumbling block before the children of Israel, to eat*

things sacrificed to idols, and to commit sexual immorality. Thus you also have those who hold the doctrine of the Nicolaitans, which thing I hate (Revelation 2:14-16).

Jesus specifically condemned both Balaam and the Nicolaitans. Why? Let's take a look at the background of this message.

Balaam

The story of Balaam unfolds in Numbers 22-25. The people of Israel were traveling through the land of Moab on the way to inherit the land God had promised them. The king of Moab, Balak, knew what had happened to other kings who had opposed Israel: They had all been defeated. He wanted to engage Israel in battle but was afraid of the outcome. To ensure Moab's victory he hired Balaam, a man regarded as a sorcerer, to come and curse Israel.

Balaam tried to curse Israel several times, but each time God turned his words into a blessing. This was actually an act of mercy. God was trying to show both Balaam and Balak that they could not oppose Israel, and that He intended to bless that nation. Balaam finally recognized that God intended only to bless Israel and that Moab would lose to them in battle. So, he gave King Balak this advice: Seduce the Israelites by involving their men in sexual activity with your women, and then teach them the ways of your gods.

Moab's religion involved temple prostitutes and sexual gatherings. Basically, Balaam's strategy was, *Don't engage the Israelites in battle, you'll lose. Instead, seduce them sexually and get them to compromise their convictions. Then, get them to serve your gods.*

The advice worked. We see in Numbers 25 that Israel began to get involved sexually with Moab, and then were invited to Moab's pagan sacrificial rituals. Even after all that Israel had seen God do for them, they went and bowed down to Moab's gods. When we get involved sexually with others, it can greatly cloud our thinking and cause us to compromise. Our judgment can be corrupted so that what is wrong starts to seem right. God's standards can seem wrong or "old-fashioned" and not apply to a person's circumstances. But His standards are always best for us. He is trying to protect us from acts that will harm us.

Today, Satan does the same thing. He entices Christians to accept unscriptural sexual standards that cause them to compromise God's standards for their lives. He is always trying to cheat us out of God's best for our life.

Nicolaitans

God also said to the church at Pergamos that there were those among them *"who hold the doctrine of the Nicolaitans, which thing I hate"* (Revelation 2:16). The Nicolaitans were a group of Christians who taught that it was permissible to accept the immoral practices of society in order to be accepted. They reasoned that their witness for Christ would be more effective if society accepted them, so they compromised their stand on sexual purity.

So, whether Christians were actually engaging in sexual activity outside of marriage (fornication or adultery), or whether they were choosing to accept immorality to fit in, both were wrong in God's sight.

God has set up His standards and His truth, and there is no reason to apologize for His truth. God expects us to adopt His standards for our lives and not compromise. This does not mean we condemn those who do.

In reality, in the world today, many—if not most—people become sexually involved outside of marriage. We should not be judgmental towards others. Like any area where we compromise God's standard, He stands ready to forgive and redeem all of us, regardless of our sins. But God has established His standard because it is what it best for us. He always wants to spare us from the hurt and effects of sin in all areas of life, including sexual sin. We can love people without accepting practices that are unscriptural.

Sexual compromise can affect us deeply and will affect our relationship with God. That's why God says in the Bible to abstain from it. We can be led astray and miss out on God's best for us.

Choosing God's Standards

The question that faces each us is: what will *we* do with God's standards? Will we accept them and base our lives on them, or will we compromise because of our own desires or in order to fit in? This is a choice every man must make, married or single. It not only holds implications for what we will accept or condone in others, but what we will do ourselves.

For a Married Man

When we pray and ask God to give us a supernatural love for our wife, allow ourselves to love her, and allow our natural sexual desires to be focused on her alone, we will not only be satisfied with our relationship with her, we will be excited and "enraptured" by our love for her, as it states in Scripture. God would not state this in the Bible if it were not possible.

The world promotes the idea that a man will likely not love his wife in a romantic way beyond some point in their marriage. A man might say, "I just don't love her anymore," and that excuses him to seek "love" with someone else. This premise is simply not true.

As a result of this false thinking, marriages and families are devastated by divorce and adulterous affairs, and children are greatly affected and grow up thinking harmful behaviors are normal. When those same temptations of divorce and adultery come their way, they accept it as standard. Families are the building block of society. Satan wants to do all he can to destroy the family and thus, the church and society at large.

Our sexual relationship with our wife, and all aspects of our life with her, flows from our love for her. If our love grows cold, then we will be dissatisfied. But if we allow God to teach us about His love and stir up our love for our wife, we can love her more deeply and fully the longer we are married. That is God's plan. He doesn't desire for us to have a love that fails. His love doesn't fail us. If we allow Him to give us a love for our wife, His love flowing through us will not fail.

For an Unmarried Man

God's standard for sexual involvement is an especially crucial question for an unmarried man. Although men have a sexual drive and a desire to be sexually intimate with a woman, God's standard is to wait for marriage to do so.

In Western societies, a single man who is a virgin is almost laughed at. In many circles, those who are virgins beyond a certain age are thought of as abnormal or so undesirable that no one will have them. However, a man must choose whether he wants to please God or succumb to society's norms. Sexual moral purity is God's standard.

Today's concept of dating and being involved sexually is harmful to a Christian (and to anyone, really). The Bible is silent about dating. The culture that prevailed in Bible times frowned on young men and women spending unsupervised time together. The reason was obvious: the temptation to become sexually involved prior to marriage, which brings many consequences.

Single men and women may pay a price in their bodies from a sexually transmitted disease (STD). In addition, years of their lives may be wasted in unfruitful relationships, along with the accompanying wounds and disappointments from failed relationships. There may be unwanted pregnancies, and even abortions. These are just a few of the more obvious negative consequences that can result from sexuality expressed outside of a loving, committed marriage relationship. The community, families, and society also pay a price when sexual boundaries are broken down.

In addition to these practical reasons to remain sexually pure, I want to highlight a few that are of special concern for a single Christian man.

Obstacles to a happy marriage. As we have discussed, those who have multiple sexual partners prior to marriage may have a difficult time giving their whole hearts to their spouses. God wants men to have a one-woman heart, and He wants women to have a one-man heart.

However, God desires to "heal" our hearts, minds, and emotions so we can have the relationship with our spouse He desires. Obviously, a person who struggles in this area should pray and ask God to restore their heart so it can be given to Him wholly, and also to their mate.

Impaired judgment. When two people become involved sexually, their ability to receive wise counsel and use sound judgment about the relationship becomes seriously impaired. If others try to counsel them that the relationship is wrong or the person they are involved with is not right for them, they often cannot accept it. At the very least, their judgment is seriously impaired. When we love someone, or merely are involved intimately with them, there is a natural instinct to defend them.

That is why we should be very careful with whom we give our hearts to, as well as our bodies. Many people have married someone who is not best for them because they were sexually involved prior to marriage. Once married, God's Word is clear that they need to work through the problems and learn to love each other with an unconditional love. His Holy Spirit in us can and will help us to do that. But there can be heartbreak along the way. Living by God's Word and receiving wise counsel can help avoid many traps and heartbreaks.

Ungodly or supernatural influence. When we have sex with someone, our hearts open to that person and to the spiritual forces that may be working in them. The Bible says that we become "one" with the people with whom we are sexually involved:

> *The body is not meant for sexual immorality, but for the Lord, and the Lord for the body. And God raised the Lord and will also raise us up by his power. Do you not know that your bodies are members of Christ? Shall I then take the members of Christ and make them members of a prostitute? Never! Or do you not know that he who is joined to a prostitute becomes one body with her? For, as it is written, "The two will become one flesh." But he who is joined to the Lord becomes one spirit with him. Flee from sexual immorality. Every other sin a person commits is outside the body, but the sexually immoral person sins against his own body.*
> (1 Corinthians 6:13-18)

The influences that come through the sexual relationship can lead us astray and cause us to become spiritually cold. We may want to please that person more than the Lord. In addition, we open ourselves to the influence of any demonic forces active in that person's life. We cannot live in violation of God's principles without it affecting us spiritually.

In a counseling session, a man told me how he had led an immoral life prior to accepting the Lord Jesus for salvation. Those past experiences continued to plague his memories and his relationship with his wife. He found himself comparing his wife with the other women with whom he had had sex. At times, he would think about those past relationships with fondness.

I told him he had to realize those experiences and relationships were wrong. We prayed, and he began to repent of each time he had compromised God's standards for sexuality. As he did, God began to reveal to him and to me that there had been demonic forces prevalent in some of the women he had been involved with, and those influences were behind specific things he was struggling with. He had opened himself to these forces by becoming "one flesh" with these women. As he repented and asked God to free him of these influences, he sensed a freedom he had not previously had.

Please understand that, when he became a Christian, God forgave him of all past wrong actions or sin. However, since these past relationships still had a wrongful place in his heart, he needed to repent of thinking of them as pleasurable times and view them according to God's perspective. They were an "open door" to the enemy in his life and thinking. Until he changed his thinking about these relationships and accepted God's standards, his heart could not be healed, and he could not begin to walk in moral freedom.

He also needed to do this in order for his heart to be restored so he could give his whole heart to his wife, not just what was left over after he had given pieces of his heart to other women. As he prayed over this and sought God for healing, his love and relationship with his wife began to grow and become a source of joy and satisfaction for him. There was a change right away, but he also had to continue to pray over this area for a change of heart and healing in his soul.

The Bible says we are to be *"transformed by the renewing of [our] mind"* (Romans 12:2). Transformation can take time, but it is necessary. Our heart and mind need to come into conformance with God's Word and truth. As we meditate on the truth in God's Word, the Bible, our thoughts and hearts begin to change and our life is renewed. God wants to heal us and change us. As we seek Him to do this, He will. We will change, be transformed and live in new freedom!

As we pray over our life, it is important that we claim our new identity in Christ. We are a new creation, and part of that new life is claiming all that God has for us and confessing it over our life. We do this for ourself. We need to remind ourselves again and again what God has done for us and the person God has ordained us to be. As we claim our new identity and begin to allow God to love our wife through us, we will begin to "shake off" the past and live in God's love, grace, and forgiveness.

By doing this, the bonds of the past can be broken and we can live the new life God has for us. We can be free of our past, regardless of what it was.

Hearts, minds, and emotions programmed for immorality. As this man discovered, when people participate sexually with others, they actually program their hearts, minds, and emotions to accept it as normal and to desire it. When we accept Christ as Savior, the power of sin is broken in our lives. However, any area where we still harbor sin—give it a place in our hearts—can be a stumbling block to us. We must come into agreement with God and ask Him to break any ties we have to any pattern of immorality. We must ask Him to heal us emotionally. He wants to heal us and free us.

The Call to Purity

Anytime we stray from God's truth, be it sexually, ethically, or any other area, we stray from God's plan for us and open ourselves to be led astray. Just as God admonished the churches in Revelation not to take up the doctrine of the Nicolaitans, compromise of God's standards sexually can cause you to become "soft" on God's principles. This can lead to compromise in other areas and weaken your relationship with God. Worse yet, it can cause a person to stray from following God and miss His best in their lives.

Please understand, I believe in God's grace and His love. God can and does forgive. He can and does heal and restore. However, we need to flee from immorality and compromise.

Can God heal us? Yes! Can God restore us? Yes! It is not a matter of God's ability to heal us. We are saved by grace and mercy, characteristics of the nature of God. But the things we accept into our lives that are unscriptural can hinder us until we deal with it. In our hearts, we must put away things we have been involved in that are against God's will for us and if needed, we should seek God to be healed of any consequences in our lives we are suffering because of those things.

In the passages we have looked at, God reveals His standards in order to protect the churches and His children. God did not give us the gift of sex and then take it away. It was given to be enjoyed with His blessing of intimacy between a husband and a wife—a man and a woman. Just as He loves us and delights in us, He desires us to love our spouses and delight in them.

If you are single, don't buy into the world's concept of what dating and/or sexuality should be, and don't put yourself in compromising situations with multiple people. Instead, seek God to lead you to a person who loves the Lord and will be a blessing to your life, someone who will love you and be faithful to you. Obviously, it will be someone you can love and spend the rest of your life with. Save yourself for God and your future wife. If you choose to seek God's best, He will bring about His best for you. Seek God for His standard; He will not let you down. His best is always better than ours!

QUESTIONS FOR REFLECTION AND DISCUSSION

1. Is there a way in which you have accepted the world's standard of morality instead of God's? If so, what standard will you now choose, based on the passages we have studied? What makes you feel this way? Write your response below.

   _____
   _____
   _____
   _____

2. How might this standard require a change in your thought patterns or actions?

   _____
   _____
   _____
   _____

3. Based on what we have studied, in what areas might you need God to heal your heart and give you a whole heart to love Him and your wife?

_____
_____
_____
_____

4. If you are single, do you agree that you must limit your activities, and/or not put yourself (or the women with whom you interact) in a compromising situation? If you agree, list below any activities or practices you think you should avoid.

_____
_____
_____

5. If you had sexual relationships with women prior to marriage, do you now agree that they were wrong, and why? If you haven't already done so, I encourage you go to God, repent of these, and seek His healing from the consequences you may be experiencing, whether you have been consciously aware of them or not. What steps will you take for this?

_____
_____
_____
_____

TAKE A KNEE

Let's pray: *"Father, I repent of any and all immorality I have allowed in my life. I confess that Your standard is right, and I embrace and accept it for my life. If I am harboring anything in any area of my life that I should not, I ask you now to work in my heart to change me so that I will embrace Your standard.*

"I want my heart to be whole before You. I don't want past relationships to affect my relationship with You or my wife. Please heal my heart and make it whole. Show me all You desire to show me about this area of my life. I ask for Your illumination and wisdom. I give my heart and life to You and want Your standards of morality and ask You to rule in my life. Work in me for Your good pleasure."

Chapter 4

SEXUAL PURITY: THE BATTLEFIELD AND THE VICTORY

What is purity? Walking in purity sexually means we are living our lives without being involved in any improper sexual activity. Here is how the Apostle Paul stated it:

For this is the will of God, your sanctification; that you should abstain from sexual immorality; that each of you should know how to possess his own vessel [body] in sanctification and honor, not in passion of lust, like the Gentiles who do not know God (1 Thessalonians 4:3-5).

As we have seen, this means we don't engage in sex outside of marriage, we prioritize purity within marriage, we do not participate in pornography or other things that we should not—including crass and explicit jokes.

Some may ask, "Is this possible? Can we really walk in this level of purity?" The answer is a resounding yes. God does not give us standards we cannot live out. Certainly, God would not set this standard if He had not provided us with the ability to live it.

In fact, Jesus set the standard even higher than just immoral acts. He said, *"You have heard that is was said, 'Do not commit adultery.' But I tell you that anyone who looks at a woman lustfully has already committed adultery with her in his heart"* (Matthew 5:27-28). This standard may seem impossible to some, but Jesus was dealing with the root of the issue. All sexual sin begins in our minds and hearts.

If we want victory in these areas—the victory God wants for us—we have to understand the battlefield and what God has done for us that enables us to be an overcomer in this major area of life. Society, TV, movies, books and all media portray a loose moral standard and we are bombarded with this. We can either take it in and agree with it in our heart, or we can take a stand for God's standard and determine in our heart and mind to agree with Him and to live His standard for our life.

The Battlefield

Let's look at the battle and the weapons God has provided so that we can win the battle for our minds and hearts. There are three major sources of attack:

- *The flesh.* All of us have a part of our nature that can be drawn to sin if we allow it. The Bible calls it the "flesh."
- *The world.* The world is a way of referring to the culture that surrounds us. The world's values, philosophies, and temptations surround us and throw constant opportunities at us to compromise.
- *Satanic opposition.* We must also realize that we have an adversary, the devil, also known as Satan. The devil is not a generic concept about evil nor some made-up persona to

explain away things we do not understand. Originally, he was part of the angelic host praising and serving God, and he was known as Lucifer.

Rebellion, pride, and deception came into Lucifer's heart, and he wanted others to serve and honor him rather than serving God and giving due glory to Him (Ezekiel 28:12-19). Now, as a result of God's judgment, he has been cast out of Heaven and is the great deceiver of mankind—the devil. Speaking of him to the Pharisees, Jesus said,

> *You are of your father the devil, and the desires of your father you want to do. He was a murderer from the beginning, and does not stand in the truth, because there is no truth in him. When he speaks a lie, he speaks from his own resources, for he is a liar and the father of it.* (John 8:44)

Satan lies to everyone and tries to entice them away from following God. Satan is committed to try to steal all he can from us, and he uses the demonic forces under his command to try to do this.

The thoughts, temptations, or attacks from our flesh, the world, or demonic forces may blend together. We may not always be able to distinguish a temptation that comes to us through the world from one that comes from satanic oppression. But no matter the source, we can overcome these attacks when we learn to win in the arena of our minds and heart. And victory *is* possible.

God's Plan for Victory

At salvation, we inherited all Christ has for us—the ability to live an overcoming life in all our circumstances, the power to resist Satan and defeat him, and the ability to resist all sin and live free from its power.

Though we have an enemy in the devil, 1 John 3:8 tells us, *"The Son of God appeared for this purpose, to destroy the works of the devil."* Satan will try to seduce and destroy us if he can. However, by the power of God's Spirit, we can stand our ground.

Finally, my brethren, be strong in the Lord and in the power of His might. Put on the whole armor of God, that you may be able to stand against the wiles of the devil. For we do not wrestle against flesh and blood, but against principalities, against powers, against the rulers of the darkness of this age, against spiritual hosts of wickedness in the heavenly places (Ephesians 6:10-12).

Not only can we take a stand, but we can defeat and destroy the works of Satan. Through Christ's victory on the cross, Satan is a defeated foe. We inherited Christ's victory when we accepted Him as our Savior. Satan can harass us, but we have the power and ability to defeat him. James 4:7 says, *"Submit yourselves, then, to God. Resist the devil, and he will flee from you."*

Read and study Matthew 4:1-11. See how Jesus resisted Satan and stood against him, making Satan flee. He quoted God's Word and refused to give in to Satan's lies and temptations.

Even though we have victory through the cross, we will still experience the pulls and desires of the flesh, which is always with us. However, so is God's Holy Spirit, if we are Christians. When we receive Christ as our Savior, His Spirit seals us and begins to live in us. *"In him you also, when you heard the word of truth, the gospel of your salvation, and believed in him, were sealed with the promised Holy Spirit"* (Ephesians 1:13). Regardless of what comes our way, God's Spirit is present to empower, comfort, and strengthen us.

As we go through life, we either give in to temptations and succumb to the fleshly nature, or we learn to yield to the power of God's Spirit and overcome it. Paul wrote about this in Romans chapters 6–8:

- First, he deals with our ability to stand against sin (Romans 6).
- Then he discusses the weakness of the flesh that can succumb to temptation (Romans 7).
- He concludes by stating that God provides us the power of His Spirit to overcome the flesh's weakness and temptations we will surely face (Romans 8).

Many ask, "If this is so, then why do I struggle in some areas?" The truth is, though our position with God is that we inherited all God has for us at salvation, we may not be living in it practically.

Our Hearts and God's Power

One of the chapters I memorized was Romans 6. This entire chapter is a discourse declaring that we have been set free from sin and don't have to live in sin or under its power. Verses 3-4 state,

> *Or do you not know that as many of us as were baptized into Christ Jesus were baptized into His death? Therefore, we were buried with Him through baptism into death, that just as Christ was raised from the dead by the glory of the Father, even so we also should walk in* **newness of life**. (emphasis mine)

As I meditated on these declarations, I was troubled. If this were true, why was I struggling with sin in different areas? Where was the power of the Holy Spirit to keep me? I began to ask God about this.

This is what I believe He imparted to me: His Holy Spirit is in every believer to empower them to overcome sin and temptation.

But, we must *want* to live that way. We cannot overcome lust if we enjoy it in our hearts. We cannot overcome lying if we think it's sometimes okay. We cannot overcome gossip or a critical spirit if we enjoy it, or simply fail to see it for what it is—committing wrong, or sin, against ourselves and others. We cannot walk a victorious life in Christ over sin if, in our hearts, we are enjoying the sin or resisting God's truth.

Here is an important question. Does Jesus Christ hate sin? Does God hate sin? Though we know He loves the sinner, He hates sin and what it does to us and our relationship with Him. If He hates sin, then as we become more like Him we should hate sin in our life. We need to ask God to change our hearts, so we hate sin and its consequences, what it can do to us and others.

God's Spirit is committed to make all He has for us real in our lives. He will work in us from the moment we become Christians until we die. Many times, God sets us free from things as soon as we accept Christ. In other areas, our hearts (our desire center) and thinking must change before we can become free.

I began to ask God to change my heart in areas where I was struggling so that I would want what He wanted. My thinking and my desires had to change. Until they did, the power of God's Spirit to work in my life in those areas was held at bay. Or, it was greatly weakened because I was not co-operating with God, and was not agreeing with Him in those areas of my life.

We must realize that God gave us a free will. We get to choose what we want to desire, what we want to think, and what we value. True, as we grow up, we are greatly influenced by the world around us. And that is a great part of the problem. We bring much with us into our adult experience. If we have practiced lusting after women for years, our hearts must change—and, we must truly want that change.

As we become convinced of God's truth, we can then begin to appropriate it for our lives. We begin to ask God to make His truth real in us. As we pray over these areas, God's Spirit is released and He begins to change the way we think and change the desires of our heart to come into agreement with Him. God conforms us to the image or nature of Christ (this is the process of sanctification) and freedom comes. We begin to live the overcoming life—God's Spirit working in us as we agree with Him.

This process is not completed overnight. The battle against the flesh will continue throughout our lives. The good news is that as we practice yielding to the Holy Spirit, we begin to walk in victory. As we continue in this, we gain insight and strength, and learn how to do this more effectively. Will we get it right every time? No. But can we grow in His power and strength and become an overcomer in this area? Yes.

A Christian man once told me that he knew of only one Christian man who seemed to be walking in victory in the area of morality and lust. How sad! Did Christ die in vain? Is His Word not true? The problem is that many do not recognize that God wants us to live in victory, and that we can. They accept the dominance of their flesh and give up, thinking this is just the way life is.

Having improper thoughts enter our mind is not sin. It becomes sin when we entertain it and begin to desire it. One man said, "You can't keep a bird from flying over you, but you can prevent him from building a nest in your hair." It's true!

We are to fight against sin by the good fight of faith. We must believe God's Word that we can live in victory, and then go after it. Through prayer, reading His Word, becoming convinced of His will, and seeking God for victory, we can walk in the "newness of life" spoken of in Romans 6. If we want it and seek it, we can have it, because it is God's will for us. If we truly want to be free, we can be.

Jesus, Our Advocate and Help

One morning I was reading Hebrews 1 and verse 9 "jumped off of the page" at me. It says, regarding Jesus, "You have loved righteousness and hated lawlessness; therefore God, Your God, has anointed You with the oil of gladness above Your companions." The meaning of this scripture leaped into my heart.

The Bible says Jesus *"in every respect has been tempted as we are, yet without sin"* (Hebrews 4:15). Jesus shunned evil and loved righteousness. Jesus was both a man and God incarnate. His human side was subject to temptation as we are; however, the love of righteousness and His total surrender to the Holy Spirit caused Him to seek to be righteous before His Father. His desire to please His Father was so great that sin and compromise found no place in Him.

As I contemplated this, I realized that I needed to love righteousness more and hate evil more, just as Jesus did. I began to pray for God to release in me a greater love of righteousness and greater hatred of sin and its consequences.

If we love righteousness, we will naturally desire to avoid sin. Think of the areas where you struggle with sexual sin or impurity and begin to ask God to release in you a greater love of righteousness. This is a real key to overcoming sin. As you pray this, I believe you will find a strong ability to withstand temptation. Also, begin to confess who you are, the righteousness of Christ. Confess God's love for you. Confess that you are an overcomer in Christ, that the Holy Spirit is in you to conquer all sin. The desire for those things that are harmful to us will begin to dim and lose its grip as your love of righteousness grows.

QUESTIONS FOR REFLECTION AND DISCUSSION

1. From which source of battle do you especially experience pulls toward sexual impurity?
   __ Temptations coming to me through spiritual oppression
   __ My own thoughts and desires
   __ The culture that surrounds me

2. What key point do you especially want to remember about the victory that Jesus has made available for you in this battle?

   _____
   _____
   _____
   _____

3. Do you think you love righteousness? Please explain your answer.

   _____
   _____
   _____
   _____

4. In what way would you like to experience more of the Holy Spirit's power in helping you win the battle for purity?

   _____
   _____
   _____
   _____

TAKE A KNEE

Let's pray: *"Lord, here I am. I want Your will in every area of my life. Change me and conform me to Your will that I may live in victory. I want to walk out my life in victory and live in the power of Your Spirit. Teach me to walk in moral freedom. Begin to do your work now. And when I begin to stray, please show me that I may repent and resolve to live as You want me to. I confess that your power is available for me to live an overcoming life. I also confess that your Word declares it is your will for me to do so. Begin to work in this area of my life that I might experience victory and live in moral purity."*

Chapter 5

Walking in Purity

While there are times we come under demonic attack, most of our battles with sexual temptation / purity come to our minds and hearts through what we see, what we hear, and our feelings or emotions in response. Understanding this is paramount to learning how to stand against temptation and live in victory. Thoughts enter our mind and temptations appeal to our flesh, but **what we do with them determines whether we win the battle or not.**

I remember sitting in a conference room in a business meeting that had a glass wall looking outside, meeting with a number of men, many of whom were Christians. An attractive, well dressed woman walked by and we all saw her. As she continued to walk by, many continued to look or to look back and forth to the men at the table and then back at the woman. Finally, one of the men at the table said, "Seeing something is one thing, dwelling on it is another. Somewhere between seeing an attractive woman and then continuing to look is where lust can come in." Every man in the room knew he was right, and we got back to business. I never forgot that. At that moment, we needed to guard what our minds thought and what we allowed into our heart.

The Route to Sin

Our eyes and ears are the portals to our minds and hearts. When we accept wrong thoughts or temptations and act on them, we begin to participate in that which is harmful to us, or sin. The following passage clearly spells out the progression of temptation.

> *Let no one say when he is tempted, "I am tempted by God," for God cannot be tempted by evil, nor does He Himself tempt anyone. But each one is tempted when he is drawn away by his own desires and enticed. Then, when desire has conceived, it gives birth to sin; and sin, when it is full-grown, brings forth death* (James 1:13-15).

This scripture makes it clear. When we are tempted, and we give the temptation room in our thoughts and hearts, it takes root in us, and it gives birth to sin. When sin is full-grown (taken root in our lives and is controlling us), it can bring about death to our spiritual life and greatly affect our relationship with God. We can become controlled by lies and deception. This is the pattern those who are controlled by immorality have followed. But again, they can be free and it is God's will that they be set free. The path toward freedom starts with what we let in to our hearts and lives.

Above All Else, Guard Your Heart

What you allow to take root in your heart will grow in your life. If you allow immorality and sensuality to take root in your heart, it will manifest itself in your life. We have to guard what we think and what we accept with diligence. That is why Proverbs 4:23 says, *"Above all else, guard your heart, for it is the wellspring of life."* The Living Bible says it this way: *"Above all else, guard your affections. For they influence everything else in your life."*

What we accept or believe in our hearts becomes our truth; whether it is really true according to God's Word or not. If we continue to act out an area of sin again and again, it becomes a normal part of our thinking and actions.

We don't have to believe every thought that comes into our minds, nor act on every desire that we feel. We are to compare the thoughts that enter our minds against scripture to see if they are true. *"Beloved, do not believe every spirit, but test the spirits to see whether they are from God, because many false prophets have gone out into the world"* (1 John 4:1).

Satan can put thoughts into our minds, but he cannot make us act on them. He can tempt us and try to seduce us, but he cannot force us to do anything we do not want to do. He cannot make us continue to think about things we should not dwell on, or to act on anything we should not. He simply does not have the power to violate our will.

Satan is not omnipresent (always there); he can only be in one place at one time. His demonic forces help him, but they are subject to the power God has given to every believer to conquer them. Satan is also not omniscient (all knowing). He cannot read our minds. Only God can know the thoughts of our minds, the desires of our hearts, and is both omnipresent and omniscient. Satan cannot "make" us do anything. Although he would like to convince us that he has power over us that he does not have, because we are believers. He tries to tempt us or deceive us. But he knows we have the power to choose.

If we do not know the Word of God, the Bible, we may be led astray. Thoughts that come into our minds that are not of God are often temptations. If we accept them, allowing them to enter our hearts and take root and become desires, then trouble begins. Whether the thought comes from our own fleshly desires, the world's ides, or spiritual oppression, Satan has won round one.

Breaking the Pattern

When we see a pattern of letting temptations take root and ask God to change our hearts (our desires) and renew our minds (the way we think) through the power of His Spirit, we then begin to break this pattern in our lives.

> *The weapons we fight with are not the weapons of the world. On the contrary, they have divine power to demolish strongholds. We demolish arguments and every pretension that sets itself up against the knowledge of God, and we take captive every thought to make it obedient to Christ* (2 Corinthians 10:4-6).

So, when thoughts come that tempt us to disobey God or compromise, we take the thoughts "captive" by dismissing them and refusing to engage with them.

For example, one of Satan's lies is to tell you that being free of lust will also mean you no longer desire sexual activity with your wife. If you believe that thought, you will resist movement toward purity, thinking that it will lead you to a worse life.

But if you take the thought captive and subject it to God's truth, you will realize this is not true. In fact, when you begin to conquer lust and walk in freedom in this area, your lust is replaced with a greater love for your wife. Greater love brings out the natural God-given desire to love her in every way, including intimately and sexually. In fact, your sexual life with her can become more satisfying and pleasurable than ever—for both of you.

Post a Guard

The Book of Proverbs is clear on how to walk in purity:

> *Put away perversity from your mouth; keep corrupt talk far from your lips. Let your eyes look straight ahead, fix your gaze directly before you. Make level paths for your feet and take only ways that are firm. Do not swerve to the right or the left; keep your foot from evil.* (Proverbs 4:24-27)

Think of it this way. Living in purity means I guard;

1. what I choose to look at
2. what I choose to listen to
3. what I choose to think about
4. what I allow to become a desire in my heart

In other words, don't let your eyes dwell on something that will cause lustful thoughts. This rules out pornography. Pornography is sin and destroys marriages and lives, not to mention the destruction it brings to the people involved in producing it. Many individuals involved in that industry are the victims of human trafficking and great abuse and human rights violations. Your resolve must be that you will not participate in pornography. But it can also include regular movies and television shows, which are increasingly becoming graphic in their portrayal of sexual interactions. This is an area where you will want to listen to the Holy Spirit in determining your viewing practices.

In addition, you may choose to avoid listening to things that will stir up lustful thoughts or desires. This can include music that has been a part of your life for many years, that can stir up memories or feelings related to past sexual experiences or fantasies. Bottom line: you will need to choose not to think on things—anything—that will cause you to lust after others and become controlled by lustful thoughts and desires. And, you will want to guard your heart so that lust cannot take root and control your life.

There are numerous attractive women in the world and we will see many of them. Some will be dressed in a provocative manner. Some will act in a provocative manner. While you cannot keep from seeing them, you must resolve not to continue to look at them, which allows lustful thoughts to take root in your heart. Satan may put thoughts into your mind, but as soon as you recognize these thoughts as improper, you should dismiss them and not think on them.

A good practice is to immediately turn your mind to something else that will counter the thought. I have found it useful to begin to think on Scripture whenever temptation comes my way. Another great practice is to begin to pray whenever you are tempted. If you are with others, you can pray silently in your heart or mind.

As we learn to guard our hearts and take control of our thinking, we fend off lust so that it cannot enter our lives. In defending his righteousness, Job said, *"I have made a covenant with my eyes; why then should I look upon a young woman?"* (Job 31:1). This does not mean Job never saw an attractive young woman. It means he chose not to look upon a woman and then allow sexual or lustful thoughts or desires to take root in him.

We are told in Romans 13:14 to *"put on Jesus Christ and make no provision for the flesh, to fulfill its lusts."* We are not to put ourselves in compromising situations. We choose not look upon things we should not, or be some place we should not. King David said, *"I will set nothing wicked before my eyes. . ."* (Psalm 101:3).

We must begin to practice taking our thoughts captive and refusing to dwell on things that we should not. We can examine the thoughts to see if they are lies or truth. And we do not have to entertain thoughts that are lustful or that tempt us to compromise. We can choose to think about something else—something that is good and edifying or encouraging.

It's important to realize that if we feed on junk, it will affect us. Watching movies or TV programs that feed us junk is not healthy for us. We cannot pray for God to change us and then feed on things that stir up lust in our life, and expect to live in victory in this area.

If you have allowed your relationship with your wife to be diminished by fantasizing about other women, it needs to turn around. You must realize that fantasizing is lust and loving our wives is God's desire.

If you are in this situation, begin to pray daily over your relationship with your wife and your sexual relationship with her. Prayerfully read over the scriptures in Song of Solomon and Proverbs 5. Take note of the love expressed in these passages and ask yourself if this is the type of relationship you desire to have with your wife. Tell God you want to love your wife in this manner and ask Him to change your heart and renew your mind about your relationship with her. Ask Him to show you how to love her and romance her. He will.

Furthermore, we should not only post a guard for our minds and hearts, we can also become a guard for others. One our roles in our families is that of protector. In marriage, a man is to protect his wife—not only physically, but from harm of any sort. The same is true in relationships prior to marriage. A man needs to embrace the role of protector and protect from immorality any woman he dates or spends time with—to protect the heart and soul of that woman. This includes not engaging in any activity that stirs up sexual desires in himself or in a woman with whom he is spending time. It doesn't matter whether or not she may be a willing participant. As God's man, it is up to you to live by God's standards and not be the reason a woman stumbles.

Protect yourself and her. Keep yourself for marriage and help keep any woman for her future husband. It is not a matter of how far you can go with it still being "okay," but rather, a matter of keeping both of you pure.

With that said, there will be times when lustful thoughts enter your mind. It will happen! There will be times when you may look upon a woman wrongfully. There may also be times you will be confronted with pornography (hopefully not by choice). This is a battlefield we all will deal with, and no one is immune. This issue is not will we be tempted, but what is our resolve? Are we going to resolve to seek God and begin to gain victory in this area? Or are we going to believe there is nothing we can do and allow lust to take root in our hearts? Do you believe God's Word is true? If so, then there is no choice but to believe victory is achievable.

God's Strong Help

Jesus suffered temptation just as we do. The Bible says, *"For because he himself has suffered when tempted, he is able to help those who are being temped"* (Hebrews 2:18). Jesus stands ready to come to our aid when we are tempted. He understands our temptations and what the world around us throws at us on a daily basis. He stands ready to help us when we call on Him.

It may sound strange to think that Jesus was tempted sexually, yet remember that He has "in every respect" been tempted as we are, "yet without sin" (Hebrews 4:15). He is our Savior, our advocate, and makes intercession for us at the throne of God the Father (Romans 8:34). The Holy Spirit also makes intercession for us:

> *In the same way the Spirit also helps our weakness; for we do not know how to pray as we should, but the Spirit Himself intercedes for us with groanings too deep for words; and He who searches the hearts knows what the mind of the Spirit is, because He intercedes for the saints according to the will of God.* (Romans 8:26-27)

The Holy Spirit is not only in all believers to strengthen us, lead us and guide us, but intercedes for us in our areas of weakness. He knows us and is ever ready to help us as we call on Him.

As I have touched on, our confession plays a great part in our victory. When we begin to confess that we are the righteousness of Christ, that we are loved by God, that we have been given the Holy Spirit to defeat temptation and sin, that we are joint heirs with Christ, and that we have been given victory over sin, things begin to change.

We begin to see ourselves as victors and overcomers. Our thinking begins to change as we confess the truth of God's Word. We begin to think on truth, confess it, and it becomes a part of us. We begin to live it. This is not just some Christian exercise that sounds good. We need to remind ourself of who we are, who God is, and what He has done for us. The more we dwell on that, the more we believe it and it becomes a part of us.

We resist wrong by confessing right. We defeat sin by confessing righteousness and truth. Our focus becomes who God says we are, not on sin and temptation. This causes the power of the Holy Spirit to be released in us to walk in victory and defeat temptation.

QUESTIONS FOR REFLECTION AND DISCUSSION

1. Do you really want to be free morally? If, so, declare this on the lines below.

   _____

   _____

   _____

2. Do you believe you *can* be free? If so, in your own words, stay why.

   _____

   _____

   _____

3. Are you prepared to "put away" any hindrance to your walking in moral freedom? This means not watching any movies that stir up lust and not being engaged in any activities or relationships that can bring moral compromise. List below anything you know you need to put away in your life.

   _____

   _____

   _____

TAKE A KNEE

Let's pray: *"Dear Father, I know You love me and want me to walk in freedom. I know through the death and resurrection of Jesus You have provided what I need to walk in freedom over sin. Please begin to show me how to appropriate this for my life. Draw me to pray, and to read and study Your Word that I might be renewed and be convinced of Your will for me and Your victory for me.*

I plead the name and blood of Jesus over myself, my life, and my family. I claim that all demonic opposition against me is broken. I claim Christ's victory for myself and my marriage. I am making up my mind right now to seek You for Your best for me. I will not stop seeking You. I will not let Satan and the world keep me from all You have for me. In Jesus' name, daily I will seek You and I believe I will see You bring changes into my life to live as You have called me to. AMEN"

Chapter 6

Pornography

Pornography is an epidemic. It is on the internet, our phones, in movies, on TV, and in what we read. Unfortunately, it is also in the Church as many Christians are involved in it. I have counseled men involved in pornography. It is greatly affecting their lives, their marriages, and their families.

Pornography is fantasy. People are paid to participate in sexual acts. I once watched an interview of a woman who was involved in making pornographic movies. She did it for the money. When asked if her personal sex life was like her movies, she said no. The things she did in movies were staged, she was paid to do those things, and her real sex life was nothing like what she acted out for her job.

When men watch pornography, they then want to participate in those acts and their wives no longer satisfy them because they do not conduct themselves like the women in pornography. Men get caught up in their hearts and minds thinking and wanting to act out the things they have seen. Lust fills their hearts and their marriage suffers. They then begin to lust after other women and fantasize about other women.

Pornography is not just pornographic films and pictures. It is anything you participate in that stirs up lust in you. You must be honest and take an assessment of yourself. What causes you to be stirred up and lust. You need to avoid those things. I realize personally I just have to keep away from movies that have sensual content. So should you.

I have known several men whose relationships were lost because of pornography. They lost their marriage, often with exceptional wives, and lost their families. Women just cannot become a fantasy woman, nor should they be. You can love your wife and have a great sex life with her. But if pornography enters the picture, your expectations change and all of a sudden, your wife no longer measures up.

I counseled a man who had been struggling with pornography for a number of years. He went to a small group of men also struggling with pornography, who had also been involved for a number of years. After meeting with him several times, I stated, "You cannot get free of this sin as long as you enjoy it. If you like your sin, you will continue to participate in it. You do not realize that Jesus died for you to be free of sin, including pornography, and has given you the power to overcome it. You need to feed on His word, the Bible and its truth, to become convinced that you have the ability to be free. Then you need to begin to pray to God to change your heart to hate the sin of pornography. You need to battle in prayer and seeking God to be free. If you want to be free, you can be."

I am convinced that pornography is an epidemic in our world today and is birthed by Satan to destroy our marriages, families, and lives. But I want to say it again. You don't have to participate in it. Each time you are tempted, you can walk away from the source and begin to pray. The urge will go away as you pray. You can meditate on scripture. It's pretty hard to be reading and meditating on Scripture and continue in lust. You can be free!

Any area of sin we are struggling with can be conquered as we seek God and ask Him to change us and our desires. If we are serious, He will. We need to pray often, several times a day, or even several times an hour if need be, asking God to change our hearts and renew our minds. He will because He wants to. He wants us to be free!

We can never conquer sin by our own will power. We must do it by the power of the Holy Spirit in our life. Prayer and seeking God releases the Holy Spirit in our life to help us conquer sin.

So, if this speaks to you and is relevant to what you are struggling with today—do you want to be free? You can be. Go to war. Seek God. Begin to confess who you are and what God has done for you. Pray and begin to devour His Word. God will answer you and free you.

QUESTIONS FOR REFLECTION AND DISCUSSION

1. Are you struggling with pornography? Honestly admitting it and confessing it as sin is a great first step toward freedom.

   _____
   _____
   _____
   _____

2. What things do you participate in that stir up lust in your life? (e.g., other than pornography, think of movies, TV shows, music, fantasizing, or other activities/involvements)

   _____

3. Do you realize pornography can ruin your marriage and family? Do you realize lust and love (normal sexual desire for our wife) are two different things?

4. If you are involved in pornography, do you truly want to be free? If so, how are you going to do that?

TAKE A KNEE

Let's pray. *"Father, I need your help in this area. I confess that Jesus died not only for my salvation but also for me to live a life of conquering sin. I ask you now to begin to change me. Change my heart, renew my mind, cause me to hate the sin of pornography and the damage it does to me and others. Free me from this sin and show me how to walk in freedom. I commit to seek You daily about this and know You will respond and help me."*

A FINAL WORD

God wants us to have a fulfilling relationship with our wives in every area, including sexually. He also wants us to walk in moral freedom and moral purity. He has provided all we need to do so. We need to seek Him for the victory He has provided when Christ conquered sin for us through His death and resurrection.

Be encouraged. The battles you may be facing are common to all. But Jesus has provided a way for you to live in victory! You may have failed and been overcome by sin in the past, or you may feel hopeless now. But this is not the end. Read God's Word and become convinced of His will for you. Begin to pray and ask God to show you His victory for you. Persist in this and you will see victory come. God's Word is true. His gifts are good.

APPENDIX

I feel I cannot write a book on men and sexuality without a mention of what I believe is a source of great confusion today regarding homosexuality or alternative lifestyles.

As I wrote earlier, many people have come to believe—or been led to believe—they were "born" with same-sex attraction, and can do nothing about it. There have even been reports of supposed physiological findings supporting this. Many Christians and non-Christians alike are confused and have come to accept this as true. But certainly, if God had in fact "created" some people to be homosexuals, then how could He, in His Word, call the lifestyle sin?

> *For since the creation of the world His invisible attributes are clearly seen, being understood by the things that are made, even His eternal power and Godhead, so that they are without excuse, because, although they knew God, they did not glorify Him as God, nor were thankful, but became futile in their thoughts, and their foolish hearts were darkened.*
>
> *Professing to be wise, they became fools, and changed the glory of the incorruptible God into an image made like corruptible man-and birds and four-footed beasts and creeping things.*

APPENDIX

> *Therefore God also gave them up to uncleanness, in the lusts of their hearts, to dishonor their bodies among themselves, who exchanged the truth of God for the lie, and worshiped and served the creature rather than the Creator, who is blessed forever. Amen.*
>
> *For this reason God gave them up to vile passions. For even their women exchanged the natural use for what is against nature. Likewise also the men, leaving the natural use of the woman, burned in their lust for one another, men with men committing what is shameful, and receiving in themselves the penalty of their error which was due. And even as they did not like to retain God in their knowledge, God gave them over to a debased mind, to do those things which are not fitting; being filled with all unrighteousness, sexual immorality, wickedness, covetousness, maliciousness; full of envy, murder, strife, deceit, evil-mindedness; they are whisperers, backbiters, haters of God, violent, proud, boasters, inventors of evil things, disobedient to parents, undiscerning, untrustworthy, unloving, unforgiven, unmerciful; who, knowing the righteous judgment of God, that those who practice such things are worthy of death, not only do the same but also approve of those who practice them.* (Romans 1:20-32)

This scripture declares that when we forsake God and His truth, deception begins to grip our hearts and we begin to be deceived and believe lies. The list of things that come about from rejecting God's truth includes homosexuality.

Without knowing the truth, we are all subject to believing or becoming prey to any number of false philosophies. We can become seduced into lifestyles that can become our reality. We then reinforce our lifestyle by justifying it and comforting ourselves as to why we are living our lives in the manner we do.

The world around us is constantly throwing at us ideas, philosophies, and lifestyle choices. Without a core belief system based on the truth of God's Word, we are all subject to becoming seduced by any number of these.

The Quest for a Source

There are numerous "reports" and "studies" claiming people are born homosexual, which have been proven false. The writers were people sympathetic to the homosexual cause and came out with reports to try to support it physiologically. It is interesting that so many have heard of these false reports, yet very few have heard of the reports disproving them. These false reports have come to be accepted as fact and have led to great confusion. Today, all over the world, this trend of thought has become accepted.

Dr. Richard Horton, the long-time editor-in-chief of the prestigious British medical journal *The Lancet*, carefully addressed the troubles with the body of research attempting to find the "gay gene" in a lengthy review of some new books on this topic in *The New York Review of Books*. He explained after his research, "The search for a single dominant gene . . . that would influence a behavioral variant is likely to be fruitless. Many different genes, together with many different environmental (or experiential) factors, will interact in unpredictable ways to guide behavioral preferences. The quest for a teleological explanation to identify a reason for the existence of a 'gay gene' become pointless when one understands that there is not now, and never was, a single and final reason for being gay or straight, or having any other identity along with continuum of sexual preference."

There has been vigorous and very sophisticated research by gifted, skilled and even highly motivated researchers looking for a biological or genetic source of same-sex attraction for the last twenty or thirty years. After this extensive and robust effort, studying it from all possible angles, no scientific basis has been discovered to account for same-sex attraction. There are no more corners to search or consider, as it has been exhaustively researched. There simply is no biological reason for same-sex attraction.

Spiritual Factors

In addition to the bombardment of worldly and humanistic philosophies and worldviews, there are spiritual forces that work to seduce us into living our lives in a manner that traps us into a life of separation from God and His truth. The Bible tells us that there are "seducing spirits" (or "deceiving spirits," depending on your Bible translation): *"Now the Spirit expressly says that in latter times some will depart from the faith,* giving heed to deceiving spirits and doctrines of demons" (1 Timothy 4:1, emphasis mine).

Satan and his forces, these deceiving spirits, are out to seduce anyone in any way they can to depart from following God and knowing His truth. Some are seduced into immorality in the form of adultery or fornication, as we defined earlier in this book. Others are seduced into the lifestyle of homosexuality. When they pursue this lifestyle, they seemingly become trapped in it, not knowing the love of God and the truth that can set them free. They begin to defend their actions, sometimes with violence. Those who disagree with them are called "bigots" and "homophobes," and accused of hatred.

Certainly we are not to hate homosexuals, or anyone else for that matter! God hates any sin because of what it does to people and how it separates them from Him. But He loves the person, desiring to set him or her free from every bondage and snare.

APPENDIX

The Effects of Abuse and Vulnerability

There are some who seem to be more vulnerable to being seduced into homosexuality than others. Hurtful things may have happened in their childhood. They may have been sexually abused. They may have felt rejected or unloved by their parents or their peers, and so look for love elsewhere. Studies have shown that a father's love and involvement have great influence in a boy's life in determining sexual preferences. A harsh, demeaning or absent father can affect a young boy or girl, causing him or her to seek love wherever it can be found. Conversely, a loving, involved father has a positive effect on his children, making them feel loved, valued, and less vulnerable to immoral relationships, whether heterosexual or homosexual.

While an unloving home life may lead most to seek love from the opposite sex, some are seduced by homosexuals in vulnerable moments. Many women who have been hurt by multiple failed relationships with men are seduced to believe it is because they are really lesbians and therefore will only find happiness in a lesbian relationship. They then are reinforced by the false "findings" that men and women are born homosexual and that they must be among them. So, they are told, "Don't fight it; give into what you really are." Currently, many people experiment with sexual relationships with both sexes in an attempt to determine whether they are heterosexual or homosexual.

Though this has become popular way of thinking, it is indicative of the spiritual climate we live in when people forsake God and His ways. The media and entertainment industry promotes this, reinforcing this false belief, and people come to believe it must be true. The breakdown of the family, absent fathers or mothers, and the subsequent rise of alternate lifestyles, have given rise to people seeking love, reassurance, and emotional security in many ways. Without a moral compass to direct them, they naturally seek it wherever it can be found.

We all need love, reassurance, and encouragement. These are appropriate human needs and God knows and understands our desires for them. At the same time, God knows how He has made us and what is best for us, both physically and emotionally. God wants all people to come to know His love and acceptance of them. He longs for them to know He values them and wants them to be free. This freedom comes by accepting Jesus Christ as their Savior and forsaking any lifestyle that causes them to stray from God and His truth. As Christians, we realize that God's Word is true. He knows how He made us and how we are to function. He has outlined for us in the Bible how men and women are to be involved in sexual relationships and has clearly taught us that sex outside of His guidelines brings harm to our lives. God is not trying to deprive us of anything that is good. He is trying to keep us from that which will harm us.

Understandably, it is difficult to break free from a homosexual lifestyle. However, God's Word is true.

The Bible does NOT say that GOD does not love homosexuals (or anyone engaged in any kind of sexual sin, whether homo- or heterosexual). The very opposite is true. The reality is that *any* lifestyle apart from God's intended original design for us grieves Him, and results in consequences to those who engage in it—things like conflict, confusion, frustration, and often anger and depression. God wants to bring health, hope, and healing to these situations. Those aims are foundational to His character, and are His will and desire for any of us, no matter the arena in which we might struggle.

APPENDIX

The thief comes only to steal and kill and destroy.
I came that they may have life and have it abundantly.
John 10:10

Hope for the Future

If this area of life is a struggle for you, I encourage you to apply the same principles and prayer strategies I've recommended in the rest of this book for overcoming challenges and gaining victory in an effort to bring your sexuality within the parameters of God's design for you. If you accept Christ as your Savior, He is ready to deliver you from any lifestyle that is contrary to His Word, including homosexuality. His Spirit will come into your life and give you the power to break the chains of any lifestyle that is contrary to His truth. Through Jesus and the power of His Spirit in you, your victory has already been won, and He is with you in the battle to claim it!

ABOUT THE AUTHOR

Lou Turner wrote *Living Life God's Way* out of his passion for men to discover God, and to get to know Him and what He has for them. This 13-book men's discipleship series is the culmination of Lou's own journey—a life of seeking God, studying His Word, memorizing Scripture and meditating on it, and practical experience with family, community, marketplace work, and Christian ministry. It also comes, by Lou's own admission, from life experiences of both successes and mistakes, as a result of both good and bad decisions.

Lou has headed ministries, written and taught workshops, classes, and seminars, and discipled dozens of men. Now, he has put into print the things he has learned to help other men along their path and journey.

Most of Lou's growing up years were spent in Detroit and its suburbs, where he was raised in a pastor's home. Following his graduation from university with a Bachelor of Science in Business Administration, Lou and his wife planted and pastored a church for three years. After that time, he felt the strong call of God to return to business.

Over the years, Lou has served in numerous senior executive positions with national and international companies in the real estate and oil and gas industries. As of this writing, Lou is still active in business with his own home building company. He has

ABOUT THE AUTHOR

been married to his wife Joan since they were 20. They have three children and 10 grandchildren and make their home in Phoenix, Arizona.

www.ingramcontent.com/pod-product-compliance
Lightning Source LLC
Chambersburg PA
CBHW021119080526
44587CB00010B/572